Basic rules for wealth

By: Luis Arturo Acevedo Acevedo

Thanks

I dedicate this work to my wife Eliana, who supported me at all times, to my parents who always supported me and who sacrificed to give me an education, to my brothers for everything we have lived and fought, to my teachers, who insisted in getting their teachings in my head, my friends, who always encouraged me to carry out this project, and in general to all those who in some way helped me throughout these years, so that I could specify This work, to those who gave me what is necessary to carry out the studies concerning this work that today I dedicate to all of them this book.

I know that these words are not enough to express my gratitude, but I hope that with them, they give to understand my feelings of appreciation and affection to all of them.

Index

Basic rules for wealth

FIRST LAW OF WEALTH:

Pay yourself

This idea is defined in a simple way.

BEFORE YOU BEGIN TO SPEND, THE BEST THING YOU CAN DO IS PAY YOURSELF TO YOURSELF

Something that is achieved by saving 10% of monthly income.

Of course, following this law requires discipline but the good thing is that when it becomes a habit, you do not miss the money that is being saved.

In addition, "he will soon be proud of that 10% saved and will barely remember at what expense that other 90%." When you do not have a lot of money, there's probably no chance, let alone saving. But without effort, there will be no money to cover needs and be happy in the future. This sacrifice is called in the United States "to pay yourself first.

This philosophy of paying oneself first involves controlling expenses; it means spending only what can be paid for. The first step to controlling expenses is to make a practical budget. This exercise responds to a plan of how to spend and save money, which guarantees the person to know where his money goes and reduce or eliminate high or unnecessary investments.

Experts recommend when determining a budget, determine what are the objectives you want to achieve. Goals that can range from financing next year's vacations, through buying a house or paying for the education of the children, to having the necessary funds to have a quiet old age.

Whatever the objectives - which depend on the needs, interests and dreams of each individual - they must comply with certain parameters. The person must be clear about how much money he needs to save?; identify the amount of silver that it requires to achieve a goal (the purchase of a home, a car); when do you need the money?

Making this list of priorities will help a lot, because it is almost impossible to meet all the goals simultaneously. Therefore, it is essential to establish realistic objectives according to the income and possibilities, as well as to set a definite deadline to achieve them.

The budget becomes a tool that facilitates having money available for the things that are wanted, when they are needed. Without this planning, many people may perceive that their money tends to disappear, because they do not have the certainty of where they are going.

Those who have studied the subject state that when the individual knows how his money is spent, he feels in control. Consequently, the person has the opportunity to pay their bills on time, save money periodically, and avoid all the problems associated with not having money.

Key to success.

The key to success in a budget that leads to effective savings is to keep a simple accounting. The individual must use the system that works best for him. Write down what is spent in a notebook or save receipts for all purchases, to name a couple of examples.

After this, at the end of each month or period established, it is necessary for the person to compare what they actually spent and their budget. Check that you kept your expenses according to your plan and look for ways to cut expenses. The experts invite those who take this option of the budget not to falter if they have difficulty during the first months. Establishing a plan that works takes time. That's why they recommend being flexible with the budget, that if it does not work, it's better to change. What you should always keep in mind, who wants to save, is that your purpose is only achieved when you set goals and define a plan to make them real.

TIPS.

Before buying anything, stop and ask yourself: Do I really need it? . Before the slightest doubt, give up the purchase. Try to live below your income (that is, spending less than you earn), rather than over them, as most of us do. If you receive extra money for any concept, (a cash prize, a bonus from the company where you work, your bonus and things like that), do not spend it all. Save as much as you can in the investment fund that suits you best.

Prefer debit cards to credit cards. In this way, you will only spend what you really have and you will not get into debt. Debit cards have the advantage of allowing you to go shopping, or go out and have fun without getting into debt, and without the risk of carrying cash, which can rob you. Reduce the debts of your credit cards. Using only one of them and, if possible, the one with the lowest interest rate.

If you have already gone into debt, consult an executive of your bank, to help you get out of the squeeze in the most economical way for you.

Invent imaginative ways to earn extra money. Serve as a school bus to your children's classmates whose parents cannot take them, or use your home as a temporary daycare center for the children of your neighbors. All this by charging reasonable fees, of course.

SECOND LAW OF WEALTH:

Set budgets to control your expenses

Of course it is always possible to think the following:

I can barely keep up with what I earn now. How can I save 10% of my salary?

The answer begins by admitting that all human beings want more things than the money they have to buy them, or what is the same, the needs are always unlimited but the resources are scarce.

Once this reality is assumed, it is best to establish a budget of the expenses that are really necessary to do each month. There is an interesting phenomenon enclosed in this principle.

If you control every euro, in the end two things will happen:

First, small expenses will be cut, such as buying a soft drink or a snack, since it is too complicated to write them in the newspaper. In addition, it will be possible to see how much it costs per month to drink a daily coffee or buy the newspaper, for example.

Second, the budget acts as a protector against the temptation to spend money on things of low priority.

The money with which a family lives needs planning and organization that is the premise of the budget specialists.

In fact, there are areas of the economy dedicated solely to the analysis and understanding of the family budget, not in vain state entities and private organizations do a detailed monitoring of Household Consumption, Consumer Confidence and Retail Trade, among other indicators , in which the income and expenses of families influence.

Each family has its own consumption habits, for example there are some that move in a private vehicle and others do it in public transport; the amount of their expenses is different, but they have the same concept: transportation. These consumption habits affect, in part, the value of the different products, goods and services that are calculated in what is known as a basic basket.

ADVERTISING

These consumption habits in our families affect the regional and national economy in different ways, and in turn are affected by other factors such as wage increases, taxes, interest rates and, of course, inflation.

However, the relevant thing in this point is to understand that the customs that we have in our homes in economic and financial matters are relevant, not only for our family nucleus but also for our environment, and therefore a planning and budget organization is required.

According to experts in financial planning, a family budget is a document where you have the record of income and expenses in the house.

This allows you to plan expenses and purchases, meet obligations, set goals and determine monthly savings.

"This budget, in addition to serving as a financial planner, also serves to acquire greater responsibility for money, improve communication on economic matters and teach the youngest members of the household about the importance of saving, the function of money and the definition of goals and objectives ", explain spokesmen of the organization.

Income and expenses

The first step to have an organized family budget is to raise awareness among all members of the household about the importance of the topic and learn to record in a notebook, computer, tablet or any other means, all income and expenditure information, as well as the goals fixed by the family.

"Making a realistic budget is the key to improving personal finances. This forces us to be disciplined and warns of possible deviations. The budget makes us aware of our financial situation, to be protagonists of it and not just passive subjects

For this, it is necessary to establish what and how much income is, that is, how much is the money that comes into the household from salary, extra payments, and any other input that may have each month.

Then a list of expenditures must be made, that is, the expenses that the family has.

These are divided between mandatory, priority and others. The obligatory ones are the rent of the house or the quota of mortgage, the payment of the public services and the market.

The priorities are health, clothing, education, transportation and recreation. These will depend a lot on each home, because for some the wardrobe may be more important than the recreation, or vice versa.

"When the budget of the expenses has been made it is important that depending on what was left over, a fee is established, no matter how much, for the saving and for the unforeseen expenses; they can go to a bank or account in the bank because then they will not be tempted to spend them on what they should not"

After putting these steps into practice, you will know what the money is going for and you will have the certainty that it is being used correctly, as the family begins to establish priorities.

When is there a deficit?

The advisors specify that it must be borne in mind that if the income is less than the expenses, there is a deficit, that is, the family has more obligations than money available, so that expenses must be cut.

"The first thing is to cut the largest amount of optional expenses, then see if it is possible to reduce priority expenses such as making a smaller market, spending less on transportation or saving to reduce the cost of services. In any case, the optional expenses should never be superimposed on the priority ones ", they emphasize.

If the family has more income than expenses, it is said that there is a positive balance and this remaining money can be used for a luxury or pleasure; even something better, save it to invest later in vacations or a special celebration.

Each family must manage their accounts in order of priorities, based on the projects that have been established in the short and long term.

Although there is no infallible rule for a debt-income ratio, people should try to save at least 10% of their monthly income and allocate a maximum of 30% for the payment of credits.

THIRD LAW OF WEALTH:

Put your money to work for you

The idea of this law is based on compound interest or the fact that the return on money makes you earn even more money.

the topic of interest. In our life we will be surrounded by it in several aspects, when we get a loan, when we pay with a credit card, when we talk about the country and so I could continue to develop a huge list.

The important thing to understand what interest is is that we will understand how to look at it with different eyes. In this way we can use this concept in our favor or to better understand a situation.

What is interest?

To explain it in a simple way, the interest is the "price that money has", but be careful, I do not say that $ 1 is $ 1 and so on, what I try to explain is that money has a price for that person who he lends it and this is exactly the interest. The price that you have to pay to who gets rid of your money for a while. And this is exactly what we do with the bank when we ask for a loan, they give us $ 1000 and we give back $ 1100, because we paid for that time they lent us the money. So here we see how "time" intervenes in this process.

The market also intervenes here, where you will be able to know the different interest rates that are applied in several categories, whether real estate, loans, mortgages, loans for companies, loans for people. It is best that you read, seek and try to know these markets so that they do not cheat you or charge you a higher interest than you should be paying.

Why are there different interest rates?

When you are lending money for a while, a person or entity that charges us an interest must also take into account another very important factor, "risk" another important factor in this process. In this way, if I lend money to a person who I believe will not return the money in the established form, I will charge a higher interest than the one that always pays under the established terms and terms. Believe it or not, and not only in the personal sphere, but worldwide.

Even many countries pay more or less interest according to their background. And here we are going to mention the last factor, the "keep constant". Exactly what we should try to maintain is the constant and there we will see differences.

Interest rate and rate of return?

Before finishing with all the explanation I will explain well these 2 concepts that are quite close. Take "interest rate" to the "price of money" we talked about earlier and "rate of return" at that price, plus "risk". I mention these 2 concepts so that when we talk about them, there are no doubts that confuse them.

Rounding this up to the world of investments, we must always try to make investments, in which the interest rates we get for "taking away our money" are greater than other operations we had in mind. In this way the chances of earning money are greater. But do not forget that you should always keep in mind, time, risk and keep constant. An investor must know the interest well to make their investments

For investors who think in the long term, it is committed to the stock market and advises to escape from the typical ERRORS of friends or values that are fashionable.

In general, the way in which money is put to work depends on many factors that take into account the person, their interests, their creativity, or their initiative for business.

The possibilities are varied, from starting an online business, starting any part-time activity, investing in collectibles, investing as non-voting partners in a running business, or even publishing a book of your own that includes professional experiences, for example.

All forms of investment involve risks and if mistakes are made, it is necessary to learn from them. But when you find the right way to put money to work for yourself, you will have created a flow of wealth.

Many times I see investment proposals or businesses that claim to have no risk; that everything will be perfect and that the conditions are given for it to be a total success. That is why today we will see the 3 types of risks that exist in investments.

When someone tells me there is no risk; The first thing I think is that that person is wrong; and if you insist that your business or project has no risk; The second thing I think is that he wants to cheat me.

Surely something that I just wrote sounded hard, but you have to understand that the risk is ALWAYS, whether in a business; in an investment; and even in life as an employee. So today, I will talk about risk.

For me there are 3 types of risk; although at first glance they may seem 2; the first one comes off in two parts.

"The risk, in my opinion, can be understood from two basic approaches. The first, which I call academic, addresses risk closely associated with volatility. The second, which I call pragmatic, and which is related to the new wave of financial / self-help writers, puts the focus on risk not so much on the investment vehicle; but rather in the subject considered as an investor. "

So now I will comment according to those two approaches; the 3 levels of risk that I see many times in business or investments; adding as always, some interesting detail or comment.

1) The risk of the investment vehicle:

Something we must understand is that each investment vehicle has its own risk.

It is not the same to invest in real estate; than doing it in actions.

This is because each vehicle has a way to handle itself; that is why I believe that we call vehicle; and that way of handling then presents a different risk in each one of them.

Hence, many times before investing; I recommend to the people who first have an investment plan; because from that plan the vehicles in which we are going to invest will then exit; depending, therefore, on the risk that we are willing to assume.

Do not count on this plan; it means then that we are going to put ourselves in whatever investment we get; without measuring the risk; since we will be focused only on profitability.

That is a big mistake; since each subject; can and should, have their own risk system contemplated at the time of investing; but I'll deal with that later.

How to reduce this type of risk?

First of all, the most important thing of all is to know about the asset or rather the investment vehicle to be used.

Investing, for the simple fact of making money like a casino, is useless.

The only way to reduce the risk of an investment vehicle; it is the learning and knowledge that we have in it. There is no other solution.

On the other hand, certain vehicles have the possibility of diversifying into different types of risks; for example the actions.

Many times we can put together an investment portfolio that will help us in case an action goes down; we have another contemplated that can rise and to be form to maintain the average of profitability; despite the risk.

2) Market risk:

Unlike the first type of risk; here we have a risk that is impossible to control at some point.

This risk is just the risk associated with the market itself; that is where our investments move.

As much as we know absolutely everything about the vehicle and have an amazing experience; the market has many factors that modify it and that we will rarely be able to predict.

For example, suppose for a moment that we are experts in actions; we always choose the winning actions; and we even know all the necessary things to be able to correctly arm our investment portfolio.

Suddenly from one day to the next the market collapses, because there are rumors of a new financial crisis; this rumor generates that people despair and sell everything; therefore our actions are affected.

It is a somewhat silly example; but very real, since it happens every day.

The market itself has a risk that we cannot control, let alone diversify.

If we invest in the real estate market; that market will have a particular risk; if we invest in the stock market; that market will also have a particular risk.

Obviously many times a rumor can affect several markets; But the important thing is to understand that each market has its own risk.

How to reduce this type of risk?

If I really had an answer for this; I think he would be the richest man in the world.

It is impossible to know how a market is going to move.

For example, a rumor can wreak havoc on the market, despite being a rumor. It happens that many people, is based on rumors and just like that they make their decisions. Unless we can control those people; It would be impossible to do it.

The only solution we have is just different forms of analysis that help us to try to see possible changes or situations that can be repeated; but as I said earlier; It is impossible to control the market to reduce the risk.

3) The risk of the investor itself:

Now we go to the risk that we can control in a big way but that in turn represents for me; one of the greatest risks.

The risk that the investor represents for himself and for his investments.

Investing requires many factors that can in turn affect our investments; Among them are: the profile of the investor; the degree of risk you are willing to assume; the experience; the knowledge; the emotions; your monetary capacity; etc.

I spoke before about the Emotional Investor; a clear example of an investor who puts his investments at risk by investing with his heart; more than with the head.

Depending on the case, we can use intuition; but if 1 + 1 is equal to 2; we should not invest emotionally thinking that 1 + 1 could be 3; because it never will be.

On the other hand, our investor profile will then determine a greater or lesser risk.

There are investors who prefer passive investments; of low risk and therefore a lower profitability; as well as there are investors who prefer investments with high risk and greater profitability.

That's why I put so much emphasis on having an investment plan or at least having our profile defined a bit.

This will help us just to choose those investments that adapt to us instead of grabbing as much investment as we can.

It also depends a lot on the financial back that each investor has; it is not the same to risk 100% of our savings; to risk 10%.

SOMETHING BASIC AND IMPORTANT IN INVESTMENTS IS NOT INVESTING AN AMOUNT OF MONEY, THAT OF LOSING IT, CAN AFFECT OUR QUALITY OF LIFE.

This also refers to our savings; it is not advisable to invest 100% of them and in case of doing so; I recommend investing in education to have more knowledge and experience.

How are these types of risks diminished?

There are many forms; but among them I recommend:

Having defined our investment profile.

Having defined an investment plan or even knowing what kind of investments we could take into account.

Know clearly the risk that we are willing to assume; to be able to select investments of similar or lesser risk.

Train us and learn about each investment vehicle before investing.

Never invest emotionally; I talk about investing as well as doing business.

There is not much logic or options; to diminish this, we simply must learn; train us inform us; and just focus on strengthening and growing our Financial Intelligence.

In any case, the best advice is to invest in those things that interest, in which satisfaction is found, because in the end "nothing serves so much success as passion"

FOURTH LAW OF WEALTH:

Protect yourself against losses

If all the above has paid off, it is possible to have some extra money but beware, then the temptations to spend it or make new investments could come.

The best thing is not to get carried away by the idea of making quick money so it is convenient not to listen to the advice of those people who can recommend an investment.

DO NOT LOSE EVERYTHING THAT IS THE KEY TO BUILDING WEALTH

Although your personal finances depend on your income, it is your expenses that are impoverishing you without realizing it. Why? This is because when we talk about personal finances, we usually focus on how much we earn, and not on what we spend.

Do not think that your current situation is due to the little you earn, but to how badly you invest what you have.

Here you have 12 unnecessary expenses that once eliminated or modified, will forever change your personal finances; but if you ignore them, they will continue to impoverish you, and the worst thing is that you do not even realize:

1. Television cable

How many TV channels do you see often 3, 5 ... maximum 10? What do you need then 120 channels, movie packages, and how much benefit do they offer you extra?

Cut out your television cable plan. If you are an inveterate consumer of movies and series consider Netflix, a much cheaper alternative.

Are you paying for channels in High Definition without at least having a TV with these conditions? Or worse, you do not know how your cable plan is built?

Check your bill and see if you are consuming this service to the maximum, in case it is not, adjust it or delete it.

2. Bank commissions

Did you know that every time you withdraw money at the bank's ATMs they are charging you a commission? Did you know that each bank withdrawal you make in check has an additional cost? Or did you know that sometimes, by paying with your credit card, you save some taxes on consumption?

You have several alternatives: There are banks that charge cheaper rates; they do contests for people who use the card or even charge commissions. Find out how much they charge you in your branch and analyze what options you have with other banks.

3. Extended guarantees

These guarantees are those that you offer when you buy products, usually technology, and that protect you additionally. While it is important to take care of your purchases, there are some extended warranties that are not simply a waste of money.

Apart from being expensive, their terms and conditions (which you have never read!) Have a number of clauses that leave you unprotected.

The best solution is to be careful with your belongings and keep the guarantee that comes with the product by default.

4. Rent

We are not saying that you stop paying rent or that you live on the street. The only question is whether that luxurious apartment in the most exclusive and expensive sector of your city is worth it.

If you change your apartment for a smaller one and in another location, you will not only stop spending money on an expensive lease, but you will stop thinking about how to fill those empty spaces that require money.

Finally, if you are paying very high fees for rent consider the possibility of acquiring a mortgage and buy your own home. It is preferable to pay fees that will have a return, and not a lease.

5. Telephony and internet data

How many minutes, messages and internet data do you have each month in your cell phone plan? Do you consume them all? Do you know at least how many do you have?

Probably not.

Why not look for one that is more in line with your consumption habits, look for another company that provides the same service for a lower price or cut services that you do not use?

Now, if you are one of those who do not have a plan but you reload your line every time the resources are finished, I invite you to do accounts and see that a monthly payment is much more profitable and not something sporadic.

6. Internet purchases

Online stores are one of the biggest enemies of your personal finances. Most purchases you make there are unnecessary and are impoverishing you in an accelerated manner.

Not only are shoes, clothes and accessories, they are also premium services that you buy and never use. In addition, these purchases come with shipping costs, which we almost never consider and that increase the value of the invoice

Solution: The next time you go to buy something online, ask yourself if you need it, once you answer, wait one day to make the purchase. This way you avoid compulsive purchases that you do not need.

7. Fast food

Fast food, restaurants and office lunches are enjoyed more, the fewer times they repeat themselves. If every 8 days you are eating hamburgers, pizzas and Chinese food on the street you are not only doing away with your finances, you are ending your physical health.

There's nothing wrong with eating out on the street from time to time, eating out with your friends or having a special dinner with your partner, but if this becomes part of your routine it will not only become something without grace but will will affect your finances.

The same goes for homes, if you're thinking of asking for food at home.

8. Life insurance

There is nothing wrong with life insurance; in fact, they serve to protect the future of your family members. The problem is with the type of life insurance you are paying.

Regardless of which you are going to choose, remember that their value will depend on your age, the risks you assume and other factors such as your health and family. The suggestion is that you look for alternatives, for example as your credit card, which offers insurance for being a cardholder, or pension funds, that assure you by having an account with them.

If you have never done an analysis you are surely paying an expensive plan, or a plan that protects you from risks that do not run or that offers services that you do not use.

Do the homework to investigate first to make an informed decision.

9. Expensive gifts

Love, friendship and affection are not demonstrated by the price of your gifts, it's that simple. A gift of thousands of dollars will not show how much you love a person.

If what you want is to impress others with your "breadth", you are invited to continue impoverishing yourself at the point of expensive gifts.

In addition, the love of your life will not want you depending on the amount of zeros that your gift is worth; and if you do so, it is time to reconsider if you are the love of your life.

Alternative: Do not fall into the trap of turning your relationships into a simple exchange of expensive gifts. Consider giving experiences better, you are worth less, and appreciate with time, while things are losing their value.

10. Lottery tickets

The fact that you play the lottery is not only impoverishing you, it also shows that you are not in control of your projects. Why? Because you wait, miraculously, to be a millionaire. You are not doing anything about it to get it beyond buying a ticket and waiting for your luck and a few numbers to do the work.

Are you of what you think the only way to get rich is buying the lottery, and if you do not buy it, you can never do it? How sad can be the fact that your wealth depends on a lottery, and not your actions and decisions.

In short, buying the lottery is not only taking your money, drawing lots, but reflects your mentality of poverty.

11. Cafes, lattes and cappuccinos

How much money have you spent in $ 3 coffees? In my particular case, many (this is a point that I must review in a particular way).

Taking a good coffee in a nice space is worth it, but your enjoyment is inversely correlated with your consumption habit. That is, the more times you do it, the less you enjoy it.

Make the following accounts:

With two coffees that you stop buying in the street, you will have enough money to buy a bag of coffee and prepare it at home. The coffee that you consume during a month in the street is equivalent to an economic coffee machine to prepare it in your house.

And finally, the money you spend on street coffee for two months is equivalent to a specialized coffee maker that prepares the same latte and cappuccino you're buying. Remember that there is nothing wrong with enjoying these pleasures of life, I love latte, but when you do it every day, it ceases to be a pleasure and impoverishes you without realizing it.

12. Subscriptions

Finally there are the subscriptions to magazines, surprise gifts, monthly payments to gyms, among others that you never use. For example:

You are subscribed to 2 or 3 magazines that you just browse and that you have access to your articles in social networks.

You pay a monthly fee at the gym which you visit less than 15 times a month. You are subscribed to things that you do not use, that are automatically charged to your credit card, that you pay and do not even give an account.

You work to pay for things you do not use, or if you do, it's partially. If you want to pay a gym earn that right with perseverance. Pay a week and if you go every day, pay a month, if you go most days' pay the next.

With the subject of magazines, stop throwing your money if you are not going to read them. Just do not renew the subscription and access this content on their websites or social networks.

In short, abandon these 12 unnecessary expenses that are impoverishing you without realizing it, your personal finances will improve considerably.

There are many other unnecessary expenses that impoverish you without realizing it, which one would you add to this list? How are you wasting the money you worked so hard to get?

FIFTH LAW OF WEALTH:

Make your home a profitable investment

The idea that is intended to convey is that the money allocated to housing should be seen as an investment.

For example, making renovations in the kitchen will allow you to enjoy better appliances and, if you have the idea of selling the apartment in the future, the property will be revalued considerably.

Also, if there is no intention to sell the apartment, and you have a mortgage, it is proposed to make extra amortizations from the beginning.

For example, if an extra 100 euros is paid at the beginning of each month, the return on that investment will be higher, since interest is not paid all the time for the same amount of money.

Thus, the problem could be the partial amortization fee charged by your bank, but currently, many entities "online" do not establish any charge for this concept, which is essential when negotiating a mortgage, to the extent that all In the months it is possible to allocate part of the savings for the investment in housing without incurring bank

SIXTH LAW OF WEALTH:

Plan your retirement

As explained, saving money for retirement is a smart decision from two points of view. On the one hand, resources are generated for the future so that the money grows and, in addition, taxes are not paid until that money is withdrawn.

: How much money do I need for my retirement?

Do you already know how much money you will need in your retirement account? So today I'm going to show you that and at the same time you can discover how far or near you are.

Many people plan things during their professional life, but very few understand the importance of planning how they will spend the rest of their days after retiring from work.

While many believe that they will live with the money from their contributions they made while working, what they do not understand is that this money will not really reach or exceed the first 10 days of the month.

Would you believe me if I told you that you may need more than 1 million dollars in the bank at age 65 to have a decent life?

Let's go see it.

Do you want to know how much money you need for your retirement?

PLANNING

Money for retirement 1

, let's plan what we want.

Current Age: In this case I took my age which is 42 years.

Retirement Age: In this case, I took the example of retiring at 65 years of age.

When completing these two data, I have 23 years left for my retirement.

Years of retirement plan: Here I put that I want to live 20 years after my retirement that is, up to my 85 years (An average age)

Average annual inflation: I took the annual inflation of the country where I am living,

INCOME NECESSARY FOR WITHDRAWAL

Money for retirement 2

In this section, we will discover how much money we need to be able to live "comfortably"

Annual income: about $ 12,000 assuming that a person earns $ 1,000 a month.

% of income that we want: Here I was very optimistic and I said that I wanted 100% of that annual income, that is, to maintain a rhythm of life of 1,000 dollars per month.

Finally it appears to me that the income for the first year of retirement should be $ 12,000, so we already know with what money we "want" to live each year of retirement.

OTHER AVAILABLE INCOME

Money for retirement 3

Obviously a person can have other income during his life and in this section we will see and complete with this data.

Annual or retirement pension: I'm going to assume that they will pay me $ 1,200 a year (assuming they give me about $ 100 a month in a pension)

Business pension: Here I will not put anything, assuming that my company will not pay anything after my retirement.

Other income: I will assume that by that time, I will have a small business (Maybe a taxi) that will generate me about $ 1,200 a year ($ 100 a month)

The result is additionally; I must have or deposit 9,600 dollars, to be able to cover my first year of retirement!!!

So here is the first clue, I should save that amount or I would already be in trouble my first year.

The second detail is the most frightening.

Since we have a factor like inflation that makes my money every year worth 5% less, I'm really going to need 62,420 dollars in the bank.

Because this?

For inflation, that simple. In summary, in the year that I retire, in reality 62,420 dollars will be equivalent to 12,000 dollars. Terrible, no?

But let's continue with the final part.

CAPITAL TO ACCUMULATE

Money for retirement 4

Now came the moment of truth, discover how much we need to accumulate.

Average performance until retirement: Here I will assume that in truth I am a person who never worried about investing in anything.

Automatically I discover that for my 65 years, I should have 2,170,493 dollars in my account to live each month using the money that today equals 1,000 dollars!!!

Current savings: Here I put $ 5,000, as a savings that supposedly is in a DPF at 2% annual interest.

When my retirement year came, that projected saving would be about 10,403 dollars.

Finally the moment of truth.

This young man that I took as an example (Which could well become my person or any of you) should accumulate the sum of 2,160,090 dollars, to live as if today he will earn 1,000 a month.

In summary, you should save 39,992 dollars from this year ANNUALLY.

And so, we finally discovered, the reality of why we need to invest and create businesses that generate us additional income to a salary, otherwise ... reach an amount like that, can be a titanic task.

In this case, not only that, but also, the contributions to pension plans suppose a direct reduction of the taxable base, reason why the saving is at least equal to the marginal rate of each taxpayer.

SEVENTH LAW OF WEALTH:

Increase your profit potential

The last law of wealth has to do with the enormous possibilities generated by investment in human capital. The best asset that companies have is the knowledge and skills of employees. Therefore, whoever wants to earn money must increase their knowledge and skills.

The results of an informal survey among professionals, led to the surprising conclusion that less than 5% of respondents invested more than one hundred dollars in training courses. "The majority spent much more on the outside of their head, for example, in haircuts, than what they invested in the inside"

We show you how to fill a gap of up to one million Colombian pesos per month in your finances, without giving up work or spending a lot of time. Selling sweets is not the only alternative.

The career of Community Manager is one of the professions whose demand is growing the most.

Is your salary no longer enough for the whole month? Do your debts increase? It may be time to find extra income. That's right, there are different ways to achieve an additional entry and thus plug that gap that is generated in your pocket every month. The good news is that they are alternatives that do not take much time, so there is no need to give up your current job. That is why in Economy Pocket we show you a variety of activities that serve to fill that gap in your finances, for example, we will set the goal of covering a deficit of one million Colombian pesos per month. And selling sweets in the office is not the only alternative (although it is a highly profitable option).

To take into account, some of the pages on which you can consult information about part-time jobs are: opcionempleo.com.co, empleo.trovit.com, trabajando.com.co, computrabajo.com.co. Likewise, Facebook groups are also a good source of information: for what they can consult in pages as job offers, and they can review some specialized such as Vacancies for community managers in Colombia. And as always Google is also a great tool to find options for part-time jobs.

Earn money from home

Teleworking is a good alternative to generate extra income without having to give up your job. Due to its remote nature, you can work in your spare time and many options do not require meeting schedules. However, the organization is crucial if you plan to acquire more workload. In fact, there is a government page that centralizes this type of employment: teletrabajo.gov.co.

Among the great diversity of options for part-time telework, these are the best options according to the portal trabajando.com. Some could cover more than 70% of that gap of one million Colombian pesos:

Digitizer: its function is in fact to type information inside a computer. They can be data of all kinds, from databases, to computer codes. Companies usually hire this service when they handle large amounts of information, which often must be entered into the system manually.

In the different job portals that exist in Colombia, there are job offers for data entry to work remotely, and there are options in different cities of the country. For example, on the page empleodempleo.com, at the time this article was written, there was a vacancy for a company in Medellin Colombia: you could work from home, did not ask for experience and paid a salary of $ 737,717 pesos Colombia monthly (the minimum wage).

Transcripts and text translations are also other services that are available through job seekers. For example, in computrabajo.com there is a company looking for someone to answer correspondence in English. The salary is to be agreed. However, to take into account, "the price of a translation ranges around $ 100,000 pesos per page"

The position of Virtual Assistant is an emerging telework in Colombia. These are people who support companies in different tasks, from operational to accounting. It depends on the needs of each one. It is a job that can be developed from home; you can even get full-time job options: In empleo.trovit.com.co you get a position that pays between $ 2'000,000 and $ 4'000,000 Colombian pesos.

The digital revolution has not been possible if it were not for social networks: there are more and more companies, organizations, public entities, and of course, media connected to these dissemination tools. So if you have good knowledge in the subject, the position of Community Manager (CM) is a good alternative, since it is one of the jobs whose demand is growing in Colombia and in the world

The good news is that there are also versions to be CM at part time, and from home. In all the employment portals mentioned above, you can find offers for this work, but a good page to check possible jobs is in the Facebook group: Vacancies for Community Managers in Colombia. In fact, at the time of writing this article an emerging medium published an offer in which he paid $ 500,000 Colombian pesos per month for moving 20 articles per month on three social networks.

Participate in the collaborative economy

The arrival of the collaborative economy in the country has had a complicated start, since applications such as Uber, Cabify, and AirBnb represent a regulatory challenge for the authorities. Due to the lack - or even excess - of regulation in the relevant sectors, there are gray areas that put into question the legal or illegal nature of the services that these platforms provide. This is why for people who are willing to endure these legal frictions, which can even lead to fines, these apps can be an opportunity for extra income when you put your car or your home in service.

For example, if you have a room in your house, you can make it available in AirBnb. A private room in Bogota Colombia can be offered at a price of between $ 40,000 and $ 70,000 pesos per night, depending on the amenities and the sector, so you can start producing those empty spaces, and on a good weekend you could have more of $ 100,000 pesos Colombia. The application charges a commission of 3% of the total stay, including the cleaning costs you have indicated.

Regarding Uber, "Earn depending on what I work. A student Last semester I managed to maintain a rhythm of at least 3 hours a day, usually in the evening after school, and earned between $ 500,000 and $ 800,000 pesos per month. This year has been less regular, working from time to time, but in any case only in February I earn $ 200,000 Colombian pesos. But as everything also depends a lot on the experience, so I already knew the hours and places where I knew it was going well. The center is a good place and there are not as many conflicts with taxi drivers as in Zone T. It is also linked to several platforms such as Cabify. "

To sell by social networks

Starting a small business selling products can be done efficiently, so it does not take a lot of time, if it is done digitally. For example, the products can be offered in groups specialized in commerce of social networks: there are communities that have up to more than 50,000 members, so it is a good showcase. Simply put the word classified in Facebook and several specialized or general groups will come out. In these spaces they are sold from articles of beauties, to cars and apartments.

Multilevel and catalog companies are another way to enter the sales business. As long as they are linked to a company that complies with the rules that prevent the formation of pyramids (they cannot give commission to affiliate), it is an interesting way to combine the commercialization of manufactured products and networking.

Exploit your knowledge

Knowledge is gold. In the same pages of commerce can offer services of tutoring or of advice, on different subjects. For example, they can place a post on Facebook in a university group, or classified, which provide support services in mathematics to university students: the time is charged on average to $ 30,000 Colombian pesos, and each session is usually two hours.

Giving a class a week, at the end of the month will have about a quarter of a million pesos Colombia without losing much time and managing to square schedules with the student. The same logic applies to topics of Physics, writing texts, English and other languages. Likewise, it is also usual to offer technical advice (accounting for companies), free courses of crafts and some sports and other activities.

Complete virtual surveys

Consumer information is one of the main work inputs of different marketing companies and advertising agencies, so they are willing to pay good money for having this type of data. That is why an interesting option to generate extra income is filling virtual surveys; today there are several pages that pay people to answer questions about products, brands or market trends. They usually pay between US $ 1 ($ 2,900) and US $ 5 ($ 14,500) per survey, or sometimes give bonuses and other prizes. In addition, the surveys take an average of 20 minutes. Some pages that are useful for this are compareencuestasonline.com.co, globaltestmarket.com, and this is the Google Opinion Reward application that gives credit to buy online.

The accounts for the million pesos Colombia

It's all, now they have a wide range of possibilities to choose from, or to combine, and thus generate one million pesos extra Colombia. For example, they can rent a room this weekend (+ $ 100,000 pesos Colombia), give four tutorials per month of Basic English (+ $ 240,000 pesos Colombia), and work part time as a Community Manager for a company that is venturing into social networks (+ $ 700,000 pesos Colombia).

They could also get a position as a digitizer for a company (+ $ 737,717 Colombian pesos), which does not necessarily have to be in the city where they reside, and manage from time to time in Cabify or Uber (+ $ 200,000 Colombian pesos). And they can do all this while they work several months trying to sell a friend's apartment through a business group on Facebook, so they could earn a commission of several million Colombian pesos from time to time.

fin

www.ingramcontent.com/pod-product-compliance
Lightning Source LLC
Chambersburg PA
CBHW061225180526
45170CB00003B/1167